Praise the Lord!
O give thanks to the Lord,
for he is good:
his love is everlasting.
Ps. 106:1

Salesian Missions wishes to extend special thanks and gratitude to our generous poet friends and to the publishers who have given us permission to reprint material included in this book. Every effort has been made to give proper acknowledgments. Any omissions or errors are deeply regretted, and the publisher, upon notification, will be pleased to make the necessary corrections in subsequent editions.

First Edition Printed in the U.S.A. by Concord Litho Co., Inc., Concord, New Hampshire 03301-0464

Poems
of
Inspiration

from the
Salesian Collection

Compiled and edited by
Sara Tarascio

Illustrated by
Paul Scully, Frank Massa
and Russell Bushée

Contents

God is especially pleased
with simple, humble
and loving hearts.
St. Francis de Sales

Each Great and Simple Joy

For every great and simple joy
My heart would kneel in prayer,
For every gladness, large or small
But also every care,
The precious newness life affords
The wonder of a child,
Discovery and treasured hope
The springtime - sweet and mild.

For every moment bright with sun
For beauty life shall lend,
The tender touch of heaven's grace
An understanding friend,
The radiance of loving hearts
The clouds that shall appear,
And then the blue that's just beyond
To bring us hope and cheer.

For humble souls that know of peace
The praise that comes from love,
The gentle hand that reaches out
The smile of God above,
Sometimes a trial to make us strong
The hurts that oft annoy,
And then so surely, thank You for
Each great and simply joy.

Garnett Ann Schultz

Spring Just Arrived Today

It seems that spring has just arrived
most everything has come alive,
not long ago the snow lay deep
and all the flowers fast asleep.

The trees all seemed so cold and bare,
now buds are showing everywhere,
they all have seemed to take a cue
to usher in spring's lovely view.

Today I saw a "volunteer,"
a springtime flower sweet and rare,
it stood so lovely, and with grace,
to show again its pretty face.

The cold and snow did not deter
or harm its colors anywhere,
for they were in God's loving care -
spring just arrived today.

Katherine Smith Matheney

*The flowers appear on the
earth; the time of the singing
of birds is come.*
Song 2:12

Don't Forget to Praise Him!

Praise God in the morning
   when first you see the light
While the dew is on the roses
   and everything is bright.

Praise Him too, in the afternoon,
   then gladly do each chore
Remembering the pilgrims
   who passed this way before.

Then look beyond the sunset
   and praise Him for the night
When we can lay our burdens down
   and rest within His sight.

Each day is a gift from God
   that's filled with grace and love...
So don't forget to praise Him
   and lift your prayers above!

Clay Harrison

*O give thanks to the Lord
for He is good - His
mercy is forever.*
1 Chr. 16:34

Give Me
Humble Spirit, Lord

Give me a humble spirit, Lord,
Where wisdom will take root
And help me then to cultivate
Each tender, budding shoot;

Endow me with a thirst for truth,
Deny me self-content,
And make me useful in this world
Until my life is spent.

Give me a faith that's strong and sure
Above all temporal things,
Give me a sense of humor to
Offset life's tiresome stings.

And finally, Lord, make me sincere
In all I do and say
That I may build an inner fort
Which nothing can dismay.

Viney Wilder Endicott

Wonderful!

Isn't it wonderful that there's the sun
To take away the night,
That there is spring to banish cold
And make things green and bright.
That there is rain to wash the earth
And make it clean again,
That there's a rainbow in the sky
To cheer the hearts of men,
That there are trees for shade and rest
When the heat is bearing down,
That there are flowers to please the eye
And perhaps erase a frown,
That there are many lovely things
In life that we can share,
But isn't what's most wonderful,
Is that God is always there?

Rachel Hartnett

The earth and
its fullness
are the Lord's.
1 Cor. 10:26

11

Never

Never thought retirement could
Be met with charm and grace;
Work was all the air I breathed
And home was not my place.

Never viewed the Milky Way
Upon a starry night;
Never studied flawless form
Of graceful hawks in flight.

Never rolled in fragrant grass
Nor saw a rainbow's hue;
Never showed a little tot
Just how to tie a shoe.

Never watched a setting sun
Upon an emerald sea;
Never felt my children's pride
Each time they smiled at me.

Never stopped to smell a flower
Nor strolled a country lane;
Never laughed at little ducks
All splashing in the rain.

Never helped another man
By sharing what I knew;
Never touched a kindred soul
Nor found a friendship true.

Never knew my loving spouse
Could be such company;
Never saw the mischief in
Those eyes that smiled at me.

Never thought I'd speak to God
With prayers sent up above;
Never knew He'd fill my days
With boundless joy and love.

Toni Fulco

It's Spring

Spring is the time to clean your house,
Throw out the mess and the clutter,
Time to get rid of resentments, that grew,
Forget barbs you heard people utter.

Cast out thoughts, and hurts of the past,
The meaningless things people say,
Forgive, dust the cobwebs down too,
It's spring, and a wonderful brand new day.

Ruth Moyer Gilmour

Too Soon
We're Old

"Too soon we're old,
Too late we're smart,"
I know you've heard this said.
How many times the foolish heart
Contrives to rule the head.
How great another's faults appear,
How very slight, our own,
And those with homes of glass draw near,
To cast the sharpest stone.

With careless hands we gather weeds,
And throw the blooms away,
Consigning all our deepest needs,
To Gods with feet of clay.
"Too soon we're old,
Too late we're smart,"
So has it ever been,
And thoughtlessly we tear apart,
What we might never mend.

Dear Lord, forgive our blindness,
Who see ourselves as strong,
And in Your loving kindness,
Reach down to right each wrong.
'Tis love alone dispels the cold,
And warms the hardest heart,
"For it is much too soon we're old,
…And much too late, we're smart!"

Grace E. Easley

The Faith That You Possess

The faith in God that you possess
With each new dawning day,
Will help you conquer all the trials
That ever come your way.

The fervent faith you place in Him
Will make your life more bright,
And lead you on to heights unknown
You thought were out of sight.

There is no power more greater
Than faith that you possess,
For it will lead you through the storms
In times of great duress.

Faith knows no bounds or barriers
When it is deep and true,
And faith and love you place in God
Will bring rewards to you.

Harold F. Mohn

God is There

I wandered in the sunshine
With the meadow blossoms there
And God was all about me
In the world He made so fair.

In the breezes soft caresses
And the warmth of summer day,
In the scent of ripened berries
And the fragrant June-time hay.

In the azure sky above me
And the hills that rose ahead,
In the little stream that rippled
As I followed where it led.

In the quiet grove where pine trees
Made a temple for me there
To worship our creator
In words of silent prayer.

Harriet Whipple

...the whole earth
is full of His glory.
Isaiah 6:3

Serenity

The King, our Father,
Supplies our needs,
The lovely flowers
He clothes and feeds.

He is Almighty -
We have no fear,
Though danger's lurking
His help is near.

He is forgiving
So unafraid,
At His wounded feet
Our sins are laid.

From our patient Lord
We learn to wait,
Answers to problems
Won't come too late.

We go serenely,
He leads the way,
We are in good Hands,
We trust and pray.

Sr. Mary Gemma Brunke

Without a Dream

Without a dream to keep in heart;
Without a hope and prayer -
We are like stones, in barren fields,
That serve no purpose, there;
Just empty hearts that cannot know
What God would have them hold -
And empty of the joys of faith
That bless the human soul.

For Hopes and dreams are like the flowers
That He endeared to sow -
They grow from seeds, to bud and bloom,
And seed new flowers to grow;
And this is all we need each day,
To harvest love and care;
A little dream, to grow in heart;
A tiny hope and prayer.

Michael Dubina

*The hope of the righteous
shall be gladness.*
Prov. 10:28

*A friend may well be reckoned
the masterpiece of nature.*
Ralph Waldo Emerson

Forever-After Friend

You are my forever-after friend,
Dear Lord, because Your love
will never die,
I do not have to worry
You will tire
of me and all my problems,
by and by.
It doesn't matter if I'm young
or old,
whatever be the color of my hair,
for I have learned to take you
at Your word,
knowing when I call, that
You will hear.

You will not love me only
for a while,
then one day roughly cast me
to the side,
for Yours is not a human
kind of love,
but one for which You suffered
and You died.
And I am filled with wonder
when I think
to what a vast and infinite degree,
what endless lengths,
Almighty God would go,
. . . for love of me.

Grace E. Easley

The Sea And Me

I take my walks along the sea
for peace I find in this serenity.
My life that's past and left behind
is like a wave that mingles and unwinds.
Yet when it storms, the roars and rolls
are almost like my restless soul:
the reaching pounding in and out
reminding me I'm still in doubt.
But as I walk on quietly
beside my God, both soul and sea
can feel a whispered peace within;
"Keep on, keep on,
you still can win…"

Jayne Marie Riordan

*God is a sea
of infinite substance.
St. John of Damascus*

Night Flight

Sometimes I feel
Like a homeless bird
Seeking refuge
On an ocean of despair,
With night approaching
There's no safe place to land.
My wings grow weary,
Feathers ruffled.
There is no sanctuary
From the night
So I press on
Too tired to fly,
Too scared to die,
But then...
A ray of golden light!

Clay Harrison

*The Lord is God
and He has given
us light...*
Ps. 118:27

Time

What is the value of each day
We spend here on this earth,
The time so swiftly passes by
From the moment of our birth.

At times the hours just seem to drag
Yet we waste precious minutes
When we forget to live our lives
With Christ the center of it.

Then other times the years just seem
To almost... disappear,
And yet they hold no deeds of love
Like drying someone's tears.

Dear Lord of all my wasted years
I pray that You will see
Some little seed of good within,
That You can "grow" in me

To make my minutes and my hours
Just overflow with love,
For all I ever hope to be
Comes from Your Throne above.

Gertrude B. McClain

Out in the Fields

The little cares that fretted me,
I lost them yesterday,
Among the fields, above the sea,
Among the winds at play;
Among the lowing of the herds,
The rustling of the trees;
Among the singing of the birds,
The humming of the bees.

The foolish fears of what may happen,
I cast them all away,
Among the clover-scented grass,
Among the new-mown hay;
Among the rustling of the corn
Where drowsy poppies nod,
Where ill thoughts die and good are born -
Out in the fields with God.

Elizabeth Barrett Browning

The Dreamer of Dreams

For those of us who are dreamers
And build castles in the air
The world is a cache of treasures
Secreted everywhere.

Our dreams are really a searching
For blessings that can't be bought…
The friendly smile and the handshake
Or the kind word never sought.

These are the gifts of the Master
Who answers every plea
And even the lonely dreamer
Doesn't daydream needlessly.

Marian Ford Park

Wings

Oh, to catch the winds of flight
And soar where eagles go,
To leave the woes of troubled souls
Behind me far below.
I'd listen to the song of birds
And sail in endless flight,
Then chase the sun through cloudy paths
And play with stars at night.

The boundless heavens for my home,
The breeze to lift me high
To rise above my mortal bonds
And never have to die.
Knowing I had found the way
To trails where angels trod,
And when my wings could fly no more -
I'd take the hand of God!

C. David Hay

Soon Autumn Days We'll Know

The leaves are waving bye, farewell
To summer's balmy days,
As winds cause boughs and branches
To vehemently sway.
For summer cannot linger on,
Nor in its pattern stay,
Since autumn follows close behind
And seeks to take its place.

The leaves are waving fond adieu
To summer's season fair,
As warm, bright colors tinge the hills
With garb that autumn wears.
For while the earth remains, God wills
That seasons come and go;
So, since God's promises are sure,
Soon autumn days we'll know.

Loise Pinkerton Fritz

Never Let Me Go

Dear Lord You make me feel so safe,
I know You're looking out
For me wherever I may go,
Whatever I'm about.
Though I am not immune to tears,
And must accept my share
Of heartache, it is easier,
Because I know You care.

For me there's but this moment,
And I must live it well.
And what I fill it with decides
. . . My heaven or my hell.
So teach me to accept my lot,
For You have willed it so,
And hold me in Your loving arms,
. . . And never let me go!

Grace E. Easley

A Day at a Time

A day at a time is sufficient for me;
I need not know what the future may be.
Strength for the day is enough for us all;
Looking beyond might show much to appall.

God in His wisdom has drawn-to the veil;
And though we see not, no evils prevail
That can alarm us, or make us retreat,
For we have Jesus, and His grace complete.

A day at a time, for our Saviour to show
How we may triumph o'er self and the foe;
For come what will, we have Jesus as guide,
He will us strengthen whatever betide.

Alma Hoellein

A Prayer Away

Within your hour of grief and pain
That tears your heart in two,
Seek guidance in the Holy Book
To aid and comfort you.

Time will help to heal the pain
But never drive away,
The memories and the haunting thoughts
That live anew each day.

Remember all the happy times
You shared within the past;
The precious moments that you shared
That will forever last.

Whene'er you feel you need a friend
To lend a helping hand,
God is but a prayer away
To help and understand.

Harold F. Mohn

Jeweled Wisdom

I heard the greetings of the birds
    discovering the dawn
when, to my weary, sleepless eyes,
    the night was still "turned on."

When afternoon was poised for flight,
    I heard their evensong
and day, reluctant in her leave,
    stood still to prove them wrong.

I saw them swooping down to eat
    where no food could I see.
At last, fulfilled, they flew away,
    their wisdom mocking me.

I watched them soar on tinted wings:-
God's jewels, knowing many things.

                Madalyn Maloney

So Many Reasons to Love the Lord

Thank You, God, for little things
    that come unexpectedly
To brighten up a dreary day
    that dawned so dismally -
Thank You, God, for sending
    a happy thought my way
To blot out my depression
    on a disappointing day -
Thank You, God, for brushing
    the "dark clouds" from my mind
And leaving only "sunshine"
    and joy of heart behind…
Oh, God, the list is endless
    of things to thank You for
But I take them all for granted
    and unconsciously ignore
That everything I think or do,
    each movement that I make,
Each measured rhythmic heartbeat,
    each breath of life I take
Is something You have given me
    for which there is no way
For me in all my "smallness"
    to in any way repay.

Helen Steiner Rice

Used with permission of
The Helen Steiner Rice Foundation
Cincinnati, OH 45202

Peaceful Reflection

Think, today, where e're you wander.
　　Think of all the good you've done
Think, today, and as you ponder
　　Watch the setting of the sun.

See the dusk turn into evening,
　　Peaceful shadows all around you
Now's the time for firm believing,
　　As these miracles confound you.

Miracles like life and laughter,
　　Tide of ocean, depth of sea.
Miracles that ever after,
　　Will be there for you, for me.

Close your eyes in peaceful sleep now.
　　Worry not about tomorrow.
Yesterday is gone, don't weep now,
　　Save the joy and leave the sorrow.

Breaks the dawn, a new beginning.
　　Take it! Make it! Never fear!
Here's your chance, your time for winning,
　　For a new day's drawing near.

　　　　　　　Jeanne Douglas

Still Waters

Somewhere are tranquil waters
That we all seek to find
To leave behind our sorrows
And capture piece of mind.

I find mine in the country
Where small wild flowers grow
Where eyes can follow birds in flight
Not knowing where they go.

Where fields are wet with morning dew
And color fills the sky
My Jesus waits on dusty roads
Where I'll be passing by.

Perhaps you seek still waters
To help you on your way
You needn't be where I find mine
Stay where you are - and pray.

Edna Fontaine

Farmers' Market Fairyland

The farmers' outdoor market is
    A sort of fairyland
With rows of yellow pumpkins so
    Symmetrical and grand.
Festoons of peppers hung about
    In colors bright and gay
And squash to decorate the booths
    All make a grand display.

The bushel baskets full of big
    Red apple ripe and pears --
So aromatic is their smell
    That one at once prepares
To take some home to munch upon
    At even by the fire
While thoughts return to childhood days
    And memories inspire.

The splashy ears of Indian corn
    And sweet potatoes scrubbed
With all the other fruits of toil
    In crates or boxed or tubbed
Tell us that man still farms the earth
    And cannot get too far
From God with all His evidence
    Of love and bounty's par.

Luther Elvis Albright

God's Gentle Touch

I see God's gentle touch
In nature's evolving ways.
His ever changing seasons
Brightly color my days.

Ripe, red watermelons,
Majestic mountains so high,
Fields of swaying wildflowers,
Summer's sparkling blue skies…

October's orange pumpkins,
A flowing creek's first freeze,
Red and gold leaves dancing,
Autumn's crisp, chilly breeze…

Frosted silver sleigh bells,
Ice designs on windowpanes,
Softly falling snowflakes,
Winter's white barren plains…

Fragrant purple lilacs,
Green buds bursting on trees,
Rain with streaks of white lightning,
It's spring and God is pleased.

Mary A. Bourdeau

Country Things

Spring seed doing push-ups row on row,
Pledging their allegiance to the hoe,
Farmer's joy when long awaited rain
Gently falls on fields of thirsty grain.

Autumn gold, and skies of azure hue,
Winter white, and spring green peeping through,
Paths where butter cups and daisies nod
Their approval to my walks with God.

These are the country things I love,
The things I long to share,
For in them I have found the peace
Men search for everywhere.

Laura Baker Haynes

Wishes

We live a life of wishes,
From the cradle to the grave,
And wish for different kinds of things
That satisfy our craves,
But we are never quite content
With those that are fulfilled
For wishes grow with greeds of life
That growing years instill.

We just keep right on wishing
For more and more and more -
For all the things, we think we need,
Or never had before -
Until there comes a wish in life,
To which we all accede
And love of God is all we want
And all we wish - and need.

Michael Dubina

Home

Sweet

Home

A home filled with love
Is the greatest known thing
A man can possess
Whether peasant or king...

It needn't be lavish,
May be simple but fair,
'Twill be a sweet haven
If joy abides there...

A tree for cool shade,
A rose by the gate,
Mats that spell welcome,
No castle's so great!

Virginia Borman Grimmer

Give Thanks

I wake in the morning
To hear the birds singing;
I open my eyes to the sunshine of day;
The air is a crystal
That hold the wind's spirit;
My Father in heaven is trying to say:

"All this I give you,
It's yours, oh, My children,
Rejoice and be happy; return to Me love."
So, before rising,
I turn my thoughts inward,
Give thanks to my Father, the Lord God above.

Give thanks for the sunrise
And praise for the sunset;
Adore the Creator whose gifts I extol;
Remember my loved ones
And pray for their guidance;
Return to my Father the love in my soul.

Delphine LeDoux

Give thanks to the Lord,
call upon his name,
make known his deeds
among the people.
1 Chr. 16:8

His Helping Hand

When we would have some sunshine
Why does it have to rain?
Just when we seem to feel our best,
We get that nagging pain.
We labor far into the night,
And huff, and puff, and sputter, -
Why must our life be thus we pine,
And hope it will be better.

God only, knows our trials each day,
The heights that we would climb,
And if we'd put our hand in His,
We'd reach the heights sublime,
Each day His sun can make things bright,
No matter what the weather,
Just keep your hand secure in His
And travel on together.

Nell McLean

Cast all your cares upon Him
because He cares for you.
1 Pet. 5:7

Take the Time

Take the time, enjoy a sunrise -
Pink clouds brightening the sky,
Fragrance from a lovely garden
Where the roses please the eye.

Take the time, enjoy all nature -
It is always worth your while;
You'll be grateful for the beauty
That will cause your heart to smile.

Take the time to show a kindness -
Just a drop you give today
Has a special kind of sweetening
That can help in many ways.

There is magic in each droplet -
You will know that this is true,
For a portion of its magic
Will return to sweeten you.

Take the time to travel slower -
Enjoy each moment that you live,
Then you'll really know the fullness
Of the blessings God can give.

                    Rachel Hartnett

*Every good and
perfect gift comes
from God.*
James 1:17

43

When There's A Moon

I like to walk when there's a moon,
I hear the owl hoot somewhere,
The owl puts sadness in my heart,
The moon puts silver in my hair.

The eyes of night are very black,
The wind puts bells into each tree,
And even though the streetlights glow,
The darkness is a mystery.

I like to walk when there's a moon,
It's beautiful, but lonely, too,
I know God stands behind the moon
Making this midnight poetry...

Marion Schoeberlein

Falling Upward

My knees are bruised, my clothes are torn,
My face is scratched, my shoes are worn,
But I have something warm and real,
From ever falling up the hill.
I know not why, and yet for sure,
Some things there are we must endure,
And though I stumble I have found,
It's always upwards… never down.

Each heartache always brings a bit
of greater humbleness with it,
Each disappointment we must bear,
Is but a storm to clear the air,
And so as days go rushing by,
I do not doubt or question why.
The stars are getting closer still,
…As I keep falling up the hill.

Grace E. Easley

Autumn

Nature's silver carpet
In Autumn make its beds
'Cross hills and dells and valleys
As flowers bow their heads.
Where memories are awesome
Where landscapes don their gowns
In colors of the rainbow
And fickled shades of browns.
Where the chill of eve' dawns reveries
Where the soul meets deja vu
The bones tell of the solstice
While the heart longs... spring anew.

James Joseph Huesgen

God Knows and Understands

Sometimes we feel so weary
As we go from day to day,
We wonder if we'll make it,
Will we ever find our way.

But yet we keep on trudging
Down, what seems an endless road
And soon we hear God whisper,
"Take My hand I'll share thy load."

And then all the many things
That we thought we could not do
Are soon so far behind us
As God helped to see us through.

It really is amazing
How the Lord doth understand
When we are weak and weary
And we reach to take His hand.

For He, too, once was weary
From a heavy load you see,
When He bore a world of sin
On the cross at Calvary.

He, too, knew of temptation,
Loneliness and deep despair,
Remember?... in the garden
When He knelt alone in prayer.

He is God of mercy
Thus filled with unending love,
Waiting to help His children,
Watching from heaven above.

Mary E. Herrington

In Nature's Classroom

As the sunset and the starlight
by the evening sky are worn,
so with this day's unfoldment
is my glowing heart adorned.

And in a mood rejoiceful
do I contemplate its end,
for I have shared it richly
in the company of a friend.

In tune with God's creations:
mountain, desert, and the sea,
we found in nature's classroom
what a perfect day can be.

I therefore view with pleasure
sunset's soul-inspiring hue;
it crowns a day to treasure
as a blissful dream come true.

Don Beckman

*Sing praise to the Lord
and proclaim all his
wondrous deeds.*
Ps. 105:2

Wonder Of All Wonders

In this world are many wonders,
  More than I could ever see,
But to me the greatest wonder,
  Is my Savior's love for me.

Mountains reaching to the heavens,
  Rivers racing to the sea,
Still the wonder of all wonders,
  Is my Savior's love for me.

Oh the wonder of His mercy,
  And His loving grace so free,
Dying on the cross at Calvary,
  Wondrous love for you and me.

In this world of endless wonders,
  As we live life every day,
Still the wonder of all wonders,
  Blood that washed my sins away.

When this life on earth is over,
  And my Savior beckons me,
In the wonder of God's glory,
  We shall live eternally.

Getrude B. McClain

Winter's Joy

Thank You Lord
For the Winter rain
For the bare, leafless trees
And the wind's refrain
For the gray-white clouds
That hide the sun,
And a warm place to be
When the day is done.

Darlene R. Fountain

Comes Winter. . .

Regal in her splendid
gown of ermine fur,
Not an eye can ever
Turn away from her.
Knowing well her entrance,
Must forever charm,
Crystal snowflake bracelets,
Glisten on each arm.
Graciously she lingers,
With a patient smile,
Never did a season
So delight a child.
Not before or after,
Has her like been seen,
Complacent in her title,
...Of undisputed Queen.

Grace E. Easley

Against The Storm

The snow is falling steadily,
The streets and lawns are white,
And soon the cars and buses will
Be anchored for the night.

It seems to be a winter storm,
Though winter is not due...
But always there is weather strange,
That brings us something new.

And in the mirror of this storm
Our lives are well reflected,
As we should always be prepared
To face the unexpected.

We should have faith and courage now,
To scale the highest wall,
And in the least emergency
To give our very all.

So let us get together now
And battle snow and sleet,
And prove once more our final score
Has never spelled defeat.

James J. Metcalfe

Nature Confirms the Fact of God

Nature confirms the fact of God
With budding trees and greening sod,
By roses blooming in the spring
And by each song the robins sing.

His work is seen throughout the land
From mountain peaks to canyons grand...
From cliffs where mighty eagles soar
To crimson sunsets by the shore.

The seasons strengthen my belief
When I behold a golden leaf
Or see a meadow filled with snow
Within the twilight's purple glow.

Some may doubt and some don't see
His glory and His majesty,
But I have walked the paths He trod...
Nature confirms the fact of God!

Clay Harrison

Life

No greater gift than life can any give,
Save He who marks the smallest sparrow's fall.
Springtime's green and Autumn's fragile gold,
Summer's scarlet roses on the wall.
Winter's snowy whiteness through the land,
The wind's song through the swaying willow trees,
Purple sunsets, frothy bridal wreath,
No human hand can fashion such as these.

Little joys and little sorrows blend
Into a colored rainbow through the years,
There is a strange illusiveness in joy,
There is a quiet dignity in tears.
Never given more than we can bear,
There is a compensation for all things,
And though our feet be earthbound, every heart
That ever beat, has come equipped with wings.

Life is what we make it, even though
The beauty of the days is ours for free.
Each must make his own and separate mark,
For every tongue a different litany.
Nothing loved is ever truly lost,
The slow descent of evening's meadow bars,
Strengthens courage and renews belief,
…That every path leads upward to the stars!

Grace E. Easley

…you found new life
for your strength and
so you were not faint.
Is. 57:10

This Beautiful Valley

The valley slumbers now, in peace,
    For in her heart she knows,
The icy wind's the lullaby
    That brings the winter snows.

The evergreens with frosted crowns
    Bow low to storms that pass,
That brush their boughs in crystal ice
    And turn the lake to glass.

The great brown bear is fast asleep
    I hear the snow birds trill,
The proud gray wolf wails out his song
    Across the frozen hill.

December's moon's an orb of ice
    That sends her twinkling light
Down to the earth beneath the stars
    To turn it dazzling white.

And all my stumbling soul can do
    Is breathlessly look on,
And wonder at its loveliness
    Before the night is gone.

The work of a majestic hand
    Is everywhere I gaze,
And everything His hand has made
    Looks back at Him with praise!!

                Kate Watkins Furman

Most Rewarding Blessings

We earn our daily blessings
By the deeds we do each day
And by sharing of the fortunes
That we harvest on our ways:
　　　Simple acts of love and caring
　　　Gain us grace on every lane;
　　　Little gifts of heart and sharing
　　　Earn us blessings, in His name.
　　　Every deed of love or virtue
　　　That we do unto the Lord
　　　Is returned to us, with ardor,
　　　As a blessing of reward;
But the most rewarding blessings -
That endear us, every day -
Are the ones we earn, by giving,
When we've little to give away.

Michael Dubina

*...as often as you
did it for the least
of my brothers, you
have done it for me.*
Matt. 25:40

For with thee is the fountain of life,
in your light we see light.
Ps. 36:9

A Little Drop of Water

Just a little drop of water,
　　But, Oh, the strength it holds,
As onward down the hillside
　　A little puddle molds.

Just a little drop of water,
　　Glistening in the sun,
Dropping from a shiny leaf,
　　To join a stream that runs;

Onward down the hillside,
　　Onward to the brook,
That gurgles over rocks and stones,
　　And twigs and shady nook;

There it joins the river,
　　That reaches for the sea,
Just a little drop of water,
　　How ambitious can it be?

We're like the drops of water
　　Ever reaching for the sea,
Ever hoping for the mighty strength
　　Faith gives to you and me.

A faith like drops of water,
　　Full of life, and strength to share,
To carry on the work of God,
　　And tell the world, "He cares."

Marceine Melcher

Spring Fervor

I woke up early one morning
And found in my heart it was spring
For I felt the signs of its fervor
The urge to change everything.

I opened the doors and windows
That were closed so long in my heart
I knew it was now or never
So this was the day to start.

I dusted the nooks and crannies
That had gathered with gloom and despair
And suddenly felt much better
As I breathed the new spring air.

I moved all my ill-harbored feelings
As I needed the room to store
Only God's heavenly sunshine
As I opened wide the door.

Now I could see the new flowers
Now I could hear the birds sing
But most of all I could welcome
My God, like the first day of spring.

Pauline Kourian Vick

Our Worth

You may not be called
to be a great preacher,
a strong, gifted leader,
or inspiring teacher.

You may not achieve
what the world would call fame.
There may be no cheers
when one mentions your name.

But if you are doing
what God tells you to do,
then you will be happy
that He's pleased with you.

'Cause He's more concerned
in who you've become
as you grow in the likeness
of His Blessed Son.

It's much more important
to know that you're storing
rewards up in Heaven
when you work for His glory.

It doesn't take much
for Him to be grateful.
All that He asks
is that we remain faithful.

Barbara Sandbek

I have learned
to be content in
whatever situation
I find myself in.
Phil. 4:11

This is the day which the
Lord hath made; let us
rejoice and be glad.
Ps. 118:24

Share Your Day

This is the day the Lord has made
And each hour will be blessed,
If you just ask Him for the strength
To do your very best.

Whatever path you follow
He'll be walking by your side,
To be your source of comfort
Your friend and constant guide.

The Lord is understanding
His mercy will not fail,
His love for you is infinite
His wisdom will prevail.

Remember this each morning
And you will not be afraid,
To face with growing confidence
The day the Lord has made.

Margaret Page

His Presence

Each day He walks with us
Through our joys and our sorrows,
And promises His presence
Through all our tomorrows.

When life seems too much
Of a burden to bear,
We need only look inward
To know His Spirit is there.

He comforts and guides us
Through each trial and plight,
We've only to ask
To be bathed in His light.

Spend a moment with Him
And a heart will know,
Our Precious Lord Jesus
Loves each of us so.

Elizabeth McClung

God Walks With You

God walks with you each hour of day,
Each step you take along life's way.
He is your closest, constant friend
And will be till the very end.
In time of sorrow and despair
His helping hand is always there.
At anytime of night or day
He will be but a prayer away.
The faith you place in God above
Will be rewarded with His love,
And life will be more rich and bright
If you keep Him within your sight.

Harold F. Mohn

Surely goodness and
mercy shall follow me
all the days of my life;
and I shall dwell in
the house of the
Lord forever.
Ps. 23:6

The flowers appear on the earth,
and the song of the dove is heard in our land.

Song 2:12

The Wilding

Gardens of blossom in splendor,
Colors arranged as sown,
But none with beauty so rare
As the flower that stands alone.

Columbine and Indian Pipe,
Lady's Slipper of pink and gold;
Untamed treasures of nature
Are a glory to behold.

Fragile pixie of the wood,
No bouquet meant to be;
Bewitching is your charm
As long as you are free.

You bloom and die in solitude
Beyond the touch of care.
Your shining was not wasted -
God surely put you there.

C. David Hay

Soaring

I took a trip past heaven's gate,
On wings of silver did I soar;
Where clouds were carpets underneath,
Like Persian rugs in hues galore.
The setting sun glowed in the west,
To outline clouds in brightest gold,
While in the east the darkening sky
Let glittering stars and moon take hold.
When I descended to the earth,
God's promise grew within my heart
Of better things one day to come,
Of which I'd glimpsed the smallest part.

Elsie M. Happe

Eye hath not seen, ear has not heard
nor has it so much as dawned on man
what God has prepared
for those who love him.
1 Cor. 2:9

When Days Are Sad

There are times when I grow weary
Of the platitudes of life
And my days get sad and dreary
With the frets and fears of strife,
It is - then - I seek the solace
Of some quiet, little place
Where I pray for peace and comfort -
In the warmth of God's embrace.

I just kneel and tell my heartaches
To the Saviour who is there
And I never hide the teardrops
That I cry, in whispered prayer;
I just tell Him why I'm weary
And of why I fret and fear,
And I know He hears each whisper -
That no other one can hear.

In the end, I feel a comfort
That uplifts my heart from woe
And I feel a warmth of passion
That endears me in its flow;
And I feel new strength and courage
To stand up and face the day -
With a heart that He made stronger,
In the time I took to pray.

Michael Dubina

Blessed be God who
comforts us in all our trials.
2 Cor. 1:3,4

71

To Be Alive

After all these years it seems that I
Surely would have said all that there is
Left to say, about this world of ours,
More beautiful each year because it's His.
One would have thought there would be
no more words
Within our language left for me to say,
Describing silver rivers of the rain,
The poignant hush upon an Autumn day.

And yet each hour is a thing apart,
As is each golden leaf upon the wind,
And down each lane a breath of beauty waits,
One only finds with gypsy wandering.
And every year that passes is unique,
Resembling not the one that went before,
And every second is a priceless jewel,
Because we know we are not promised more.

Not in looking, but in what we see,
Herein lies the magic of it all.
Not what happens, strange as it may seem,
But only what the heart and mind recall,
Can fill our hearts with happiness or pain,
But this is not the goal for which we strive,
We have to lean upon the Lord to learn
. . . Just what it's like to really be alive!

Grace E. Easley

*Let the heavens
be glad, and
the earth rejoice…*
1 Chr. 16:31

Faith

As dawn breaks o'er the horizon
sending glorious rays abroad
as the gentle breeze of morning
brings word of our risen Lord

No matter what the burden
He is there to share your load,
with a steady hand to guide you
as you tread your weary road.

Fear not what lies before you
you need never walk alone
if you simply put your hand in His
and rejoice in the faith you have known.

George T. Macintyre

For we walk by
faith,
not by sight.
2 Cor. 5:7

Peace

Peace in my heart - this is my prayer
Quiet contentment, to have and to share,
Each new tomorrow, blessed and real
Each wondrous dawning, a daybreak ideal.

Peace in my home, this I would ask
Sharing each burden, to lighten our task,
Laughter abundant, so much that's worthwhile
Faith, hope and courage - a bright happy smile.

Peace in this country, this is my dream
Peace we might cherish - joyous, supreme,
No more of hatred, no more of crime
Peacefulness only, in your heart and mine.

Peace in our world, this is my prayer
With one God to guide us, and one God to care,
All of us neighbors, then surely we'll see
That peace is the answer to eternity.

Garnett Ann Schultz

75

Spring Awakening

Sometimes springtime misbehaves
Still she gets poetic raves,
When she leaves her door ajar -
Spring is so spectacular.

Springtime is a potpourri
A fragrant flowery guarantee,
That budding trees will have a yen -
To put on leafy dress again.

Scenic spring is all abloom
Scented with lilac perfume,
Cobalt skies are rainbow-hued -
After a rainy interlude.

Springtime's always unsurpassed
Though she's sometimes overcast,
Enchanting us in her debut -
Inviting us life to renew.

In disbelief I gaze at spring
And know God sent this awakening.

Nora M. Bozeman

I Thank You

Lord, I thank You for this brand new day
That You've bestowed on me,
I thank You for Your song birds
That 'light upon Your trees.

I thank You for Your sunbeams
That shine upon my face,
But most of all I thank You
For Your ever loving grace.

For the mountains and the rivers
And the early morning dew,
For all the things You've put on earth,
My Lord I do thank You.

And Lord my greatest gratitude
Of all the things You do,
Was my choice to have eternal life,
For this, dear Lord, thank You.

Albert N. Theel

My Task

What can I do for the Master?
I'm only one person you see!
My talents are not very many,
But all of them, Lord, are from Thee.
What can I do for the Master,
There's so much to be done you see;
But I sorely remember His counsel -
"What's done for others, is done for Me."
What can I do for the Master,
He who has done so much for me?
I can do little things around me,
That others the need fail to see.
What can I do for my Master,
He who gave His life for me?
I can only use all my talents to serve Him,
That others find His salvation free.

Nell McLean

Let your light shine before
men, that they may see
your good works and give
glory to your Father
who is in heaven.
Matt. 5:16

78

Seeds of Faith

Try each day to do some deed
That fills another's earnest need.

Wear a smile that shows you care,
And take it with you everywhere.

Lift folks up, don't cut them down
As you go about the town.

Look for the good and not the bad,
And try to make a sad heart glad.

Try to brighten someone's day
And share your faith along the way.

Share the love God's given you,
And give Him praise in all you do.

Sow seeds of faith wher'ere you go
And know that God will make them grow.

Clay Harrison

*With faith the size
of a mustard seed,
nothing shall
be impossible.*
Matt. 17:20

Behold each moment of today -
It will not pass again this way.
Dr. Bruno C. Schmidt

A Perfect Dream

Lord You scattered wild flowers
across the mountains wide,
and flow the beautiful waterfall
down the mountainside.

You made the lofty mountains
and covered the peaks with snow,
You hung the rain clouds
to cleanse the air and earth below.

You sail Your silver clouds
across Your sky of blue,
and in the morning sunshine
I see Your diamond dew.

You hung the golden sun
up o'er the silver sea,
to shine on dancing waters
that sparkle there for me.

You set the jeweled lakes
in mountains cool and green,
and added rainbows and sunsets
to make a perfect dream.

Mildred McCoy

A Wee Lad's Question

At the kitchen window feeder
Activity was rife;
The birds had come to dinner
And it was quite a sight.

There were large and there
were small birds
With feathers drab and bright;
They were chirping, loudly chirping,
They seemed so impolite.

Just then I heard this question
From a wee lad with me there:
"Before the birds eat dinner,
Don't they say a birdie prayer?"

Loise Pinkerton Fritz

...And a little child
shall lead them.
Isaiah 11:6

Every Newborn Day

Every dawn is new beginning
For some journey you would make;
Every day is Heaven's blessing
To amend some past mistake;
It is also Grace for loving
And to make amends, at knee,
And to be the kind of person
That you know that you should be.

But, it quickly dawns and passes -
As so many days before -
(When you only wished and waited
For the things you still implore)
It's a newborn day for living,
To begin what you would do -
Or be added to the others
That you wished and waited through.

Michael Dubina

I Do Not Ask

I do not ask for riches
I have wealth beyond compare,
The summer sun, the winter snow
The fragrant springtime air,
I've trees and hills and clear blue skies
The stars I love so much,
I've autumn mountains, red and gold
Blessed by the Master's touch.

I do not ask for anything
But what my God might send,
I've little things and shining stars
A dear and worthwhile friend,
How could I ask a greater wealth
Than just one glowing dawn,
The sun that steals across the skies
When night at last is gone.

I do not ask for treasures
For I know I'm truly blessed,
With friends and loved ones ever near
A world of happiness,
My heart knows peace and quiet bliss,
Serenity, my own,
My soul knows joys and sweet content
In hours I spend alone.

I do not ask a thing of life
But what I truly earn,
'Tis still enough that dreams are mine
A tender heart to yearn,
A hope, a faith, a trust ideal
With eyes that look above,
I do not ask, God gave me all
Because He gave me love.

Garnett Ann Schultz

For this is the message you have heard from the beginning: we should love one another.

1 John 3:11

Letters From Home

When you wander from the home-place
    Searching for your star,
Letters from home will cheer you up
    However far you are.
It's nice to know your loved ones
    Hold you in their heart,
And you never feel that you're alone
    Although you are apart.

The Savior sends His love each day
    Wherever we may be,
And He's given us the Bible
    To guide us constantly.
Wherever we may wander,
    However far we roam,
The Savior wants to keep in touch
    With letters from home!

Clay Harrison

Beloved, let us love one another;
because love is of God; everyone
who loves is born of God
and knows God.
1 John 4:7

Getting A Little Older

I'm getting a little older, Lord,
And not quite so agile and free,
Yet, Heavenly Father, You promised
I could still be a fruit-bearing tree.

So I'll smile a little bit broader,
To hide the wrinkles of time,
And I'll think kind thoughts of everyone,
For we all have a hill to climb.

And all of us are neighbors
Who long for kindness and caring,
And so I commit myself to be
Understanding, and cheerful and sharing.

Helen Neimy

*They shall still bring forth
fruit in old age.*
Ps. 92:14

We Thank Thee...

We thank Thee, blessed Master,
For the quiet of the night;
For the stillness and the calmness
That brings Thy presence into sight...

We thank Thee, blessed Master,
For Thy goodness and Thy grace;
For Thy gentleness and kindness,
And the warmth of Thy embrace...

We thank Thee, blessed Master,
For Thy rapture and Thy peace;
For Thy mercy and Thy caring
That make all our troubles cease...

We thank Thee, blessed Master,
For the brightness of the day;
For the sunshine and the rainbows
That help chase the clouds away...

We thank Thee, blessed Master
For the beauty of Thy love;
For Thy charity and blessings;
Oh send us guidance from above!

Hope C. Oberhelman

I Thank You, Lord

I thank You for Your goodness, Lord,
In all the years gone by.
Through all my joys and sorrows
Your help was always nigh.
I thank You for the friends sincere
I met on life's highway.
I thank You for the rising sun
That gladdens each new day.
I thank You for the soft south winds
That sing among the trees,
They tell of fruitful harvest times
And shimmering summer seas.
I thank You for the stars that shine
To brighten each long night
True signs of Your unceasing care,
Great Lord of Power and Might.

Father Thomas Foy

There Is A Place

There is a place where I can go
and talk to one who loves me so,
There is a place where I can be
where no one else can bother me;

There is a place where once I've been
I long to go back there again,
A place alone in secret prayer --
and Jesus always meets me there;

We spend our time in conversation
In this place there's no condemnation,
This is a place so easy to find
and I can go there anytime;

This is a place of sweet release,
where Jesus gives me comfort and peace;
And when life becomes too hard to face --
I simply remember -- There Is A Place!

Vickie Swarringin

I Cannot Do Without Thee

I cannot do without Thee, Lord,
I have no strength to stand;
No goodness of my own to help
To walk as Thou hast planned.

I have no wisdom of my own
To do Thy holy will;
But Thou, Lord Jesus, art my all,
By Thee, I can fulfill.

I have no sight to see my way
Down through the years of time;
But I shall trust Thee, fill me, Lord;
I Thee my all resign.

Alma Hoellein

When the cares of my heart are many,
thy consolations cheer my soul.
Ps. 94:19

I Heard My Master Say to Me

I heard my Master say to me
"Come unto Me my child
I'll make your life both light and free,
I'll make your life worthwhile.

If you would now invite Me in,
I'll come into your heart,
The bond would be both strong and true
We'll never, never part;

You'll never have to worry,
You'll never be alone.
Oh! child of Mine, I love you,
I'll take you as My own."

I answered Him with outstretched arms,
I gave my life to Him
My heart is happy and content
Since Jesus lives within.

Nancy M. Smith

*Come to Me all of you
who are burdened and
I will give you rest.*
Matt. 11:28

A Country Road

Riding down a country road
    The pebbles crunch with sound,
The way lies straight before us,
    Contentment can be found.

The sky is a blue curtain
    Embroidered with white lace,
Flowers by the wayside
    Perfume us with their grace.

The trees lift arms of beauty
    In prayer to God on high,
The air is sweet with grasses
    Which wave as we go by.

The corn is graceful in the wind,
    The soybeans show their green,
It's just a ride in the country,
    But, oh, how much it can mean.

             Lois Tiffany

The Race Of Life

Have you ever watched the runners
As they ready at the line;
Their bodies tense, their muscles flexed,
Just one thing on their mind.

We must be strong, we must fulfill
The desire in our heart,
To win this race, our greatest goal
And finish what we start.

Not unlike the race we run
On each and every day,
To put God first within our lives
Is what we all should pray.

Tho' weary at the very end,
I'm sure we all will be;
Our Savior's gift, eternal life -
His reward for you and me.

Albert N. Theel

$\mathcal{G}$reat and wonderful are your works,
Lord God almighty.
Just and true are your ways,
O King of the Nations.

Rev. 15:3

Little Gems of Glory

God's wonders are not always seen
In large majestic things,
They're also found in little gems
Of glory that life brings:

The caroling birds at break of day,
A shining butterfly,
A little patch of tulips that
Reach up to springtime's sky.

The dainty twinkling violets
Upon my windowsill,
The brilliant glow my eyes behold
Of poppies on a hill.

A baby's smile, a mother's prayer,
A kitten soft and sweet,
The painted leaves of autumn time
That swirl around my feet.

Each snowflake's intricate design,
The beauty as they fall,
A redbird mid a snow-clad tree -
Such glory in it all!

A glimpse of heaven I can see
In wonders small and dear,
For little gems of glory bring
God's Presence very near.

Beverly J. Anderson

Faith, Prayer, and Effort... Abundance

We all at times feel weary
And in emptiness seem lost,
But if sometimes the blindness lingers,
Then we each must pay the cost.
Oh, it's easy to say God will listen
And relieve us of burden and pain,
But without the sweet gift of prayer,
There will be no rejoicing in gain.
So roll up your sleeves and surrender,
Then polish your faith to believe
That with faith, with effort, and prayer,
God will see that you fully receive.
They say the sky is the limit,
But only if we stay on course
Will we reap the fruit of abundance,
Where all heaven's angels rejoice.
So to all who have truly decided
To enroll in the great school of life,
Please believe that effort is worth it,
To make all your dreams turn out right.

Chris Zambernard

All These God Gives To Me

He grants me hope and courage
To face each dawning day.
He gives me faith to carry on
When failure comes my way.

He grants to me forgiveness
For sins and wrongs I do.
He gives me inspiration
To face my trials anew.

He strengthens and sustains me
In sorrow and despair.
Whene'er I need a helping hand
I always find Him there.

He shows His great compassion
Unworthy that I be.
Despite all my shortcomings
I know that He loves me.

Harold F. Mohn

*The Lord is my strength
and my shield.*
Ps. 28:7

Sweet Life

Life is so sweet
How can I repay
For all of the joys
I reap day by day.
The beauty of Nature
I steal by the hours
The aura of God
The soul holds and devours.
There are sweet moments
That live in my heart
And all thro' a lifetime
We're never apart.
We have but to note them
This beautiful place
Full of God's blessings
And filled with His grace.
I thank You so, Father
For all the gifts You bestow
So that in my heart
Love continues to grow.

James Joseph Huesgen

Evening Prayer

Oh Saviour, hear our evening prayer,
    And bless us while we sleep.
We ask Thy presence through the night,
    Thy tender watch to keep.

For those through sorrow, or in pain,
    On beds of fever lie;
We pray that they may feel the wings
    Of angels drawing nigh.

The sinner in the tempter's snare,
    This night may drift from thee;
Oh still the tumult in his soul,
    And calm the troubled sea.

Oh thou whom yet unseen, we love;
    Oh Lamb who gavest all
Thy blest compassion oh may we know
    When life's dark shadows fall.

When morning dawns in Realms on high,
    We then behold Thy face;
And kneel in rapture to receive
    The fullness of Thy grace!

              Sancie Earman King

There's a wideness in God's mercy
like the wideness of the sea,
There is kindness in His justice
which is more than liberty.
For the love of God is broader
than the measure of man's mind,
And the heart of the Eternal
is most wonderfully kind.

Frederick William Faber

God's mercies are never ending.
They are renewed every morning.
His faithfulness is great.
Lam. 3:22,23

Like Ships At Sea

Like the ships that sail the oceans
    We - who walk upon the land -
Are, forever, tried and challenged
    By the storms of life's demands;
Every tempest of temptation
    Is a test to Christian way
And a tempt to change direction
    From the goals for which we pray.

We are tossed and torn by struggles -
    Like the ships that vie with tides -
And our faith, in God, is tested:
    Questioned! Challenged! Strained and tried.
For He leaves - to us - the choosing
    Of the waters we would sail
And the choice of many courses
    Full of blessings - or travail.

Michael Dubina

You Didn't See

When your neighbor needs a helping hand,
Do your cheerfully agree
To stop and help, or do you just
Pretend... you didn't see?

And when your friends are troubled to
A very great degree,
Do you share your love and warmth, or just
Pretend... you didn't see?

Do you listen to the Spirit, when
He tells you how to be
Aware of others' needs, or just
Pretend... you didn't see?

But when in death, you reach God's gate,
And try to find the key,
Will you wonder, then, if He will just
Pretend... He didn't see?

Sister Miriam Barker, C.D.S.

Copy Cat

Dear Lord, I want to imitate
Everything You do,
To follow in Your footsteps
And Your ways, my whole life through.
I want to grow in goodness,
And in patience and in care,
To be a mirror of Your love,
To people everywhere.

Lord, make me slow to anger,
And let me never say
Words that hurt somebody else,
Help me to find a way
To soften someone's sorrow,
The way You did, and that
My whole life long You'll let me be,
. . . Your little copy cat.

Grace E. Easley

*Jesus meek and
humble of heart,
make my heart
like unto thine...*

Living In The Now

I live in the now
for the past is gone.
Some things I did right,
and some things I did wrong.
When tomorrow comes
it will be today,
And I've learned many lessons
along the way.

Friend, do not dwell on the yesterdays
as I have so often done,
Nor worry about tomorrow
for tomorrow may never come.
Just live in the now
and soon you will see --
What worried you most
was never to be.

Helen Parker

Your Gentle Touch

I flew across your sky today,
and saw such beauty all the way --
Majestic mountains, capped with snow,
and rich, green valleys far below.

I saw your painted desert's sand,
and endless miles of barren land.
At times the clouds would hide my view.
(They held a certain beauty too.)

I saw rivers, streams, and lakes,
and winding roads that curved like snakes.
Countless cities, large and small,
and rich farmlands -- I saw them all!

As I beheld this awesome view,
my thoughts, dear God, were all of You.
You gave such beauty to this land
with a gentle touch of Your hand!

Doris A. Orth

God's Ray of Sunshine

Keep God's Ray of Sunshine
Cradled in your heart;
Every hour of every day
Let it be a part.
That when the day is sunless
And skies have lost their blue,
This Lovely Ray of Sunshine
Will keep a-shining through.

Keep God's Ray of Sunshine
Safely tucked away;
In the confines of your heart
Let it every stay.
That when the rains fall heavy
And storms come by the way,
Dispelled will be the darkness
As forth will shine God's Ray.

Loise Pinkerton Fritz

Then spoke Jesus again saying,
"I am the light of the world:
he that follows me shall
not walk in darkness, but
shall have the light of life."
John 8:12

Where Seagulls Cry!

I love a place where seagulls cry,
Where meets the glistening sea with sky;
Where one can search for shells and such,
Where one can feel the ocean's touch!

To walk upon the whitened sand,
While clinging to a loved one's hand!
To sense the wonder of a place,
Where marks of care are soon erased.

Although I know I can't be there,
I go on whispering wings of prayer;
To seashore with its splendorous view,
Which succors, strengthens and renews.

Oh Maker of the sand and sea,
May I return in memory;
To where I'll glimpse the ocean's foam!
To where such treasured joys I've known!

Sancie Earman King

Glory in His Holy Name;
rejoice, O hearts that
seek the Lord.
1 Chr. 16:10

One Little Visit

Just a tiny little visit,
It would mean so much to Him,
Right now the Church is empty,
And all the lights are dim.
You would have a chance to really talk,
And say what's on you mind,
Don't make excuses, saying that
You just don't have the time.

If your cross is getting heavy,
He will always lend a hand,
No matter what has happened,
He's sure to understand.
You can make the time for others,
And it doesn't bother you,
Why can't you stop tonight and make
some time for Jesus, too?

Nobody cares about you,
The way He does, you know,
And His arms are always open,
When you have no place to go.
Nobody knows the future,
Or the detours we must take,
This little visit might just be
. . . The last one you will make!

Grace E. Easley

The Lonely Road

I walk a lonely road with God
Who clasps my trembling hand
And bids me past my farthest dreams
To seek a distant Land.

The silent woodland of my heart
Dares not speak, and break the spell
Of dappled sunbeams piercing through
To show where God would dwell.

Speak softly, Lord, no, whisper what
My soul must hear in prayer,
Lest the grandeur of Your Voice may prove
Too much for me to bear.

Each leaf and limb feels ecstasy -
Your love, like music, plays
Upon the woodland of my soul,
Which trembles 'neath Your gaze.

New days, new years, must dawn, I know,
Now challenge lies ahead -
I walk a lonely road with God . . .
And go where I am led.

Sister Miriam Barker, C.D.S.

*Lord, lead me to do
Your will. Make Your
way plain for me
to follow.*
Ps. 5:8

Try Again

When you fail and get discouraged
    And you feel that all is vain,
There's a second chance before you
    Stand up tall... and try again.

In the heart of every Christian
    There is often pain and sorrow,
When you fall along the wayside
    Just look up... and face tomorrow.

For there is so much forgiveness
    In the heart of God above,
And the Savior went to Calvary
    Dying there for us in love.

Even though we disappoint Him
    And we cause Him grief and pain,
There's a second chance before us
    Stand up tall... and try again.

When we look at other people
    Often judging what they do,
On our knees we should be praying
    They would start afresh... anew.

For the Savior in His mercy
    Gives a second chance to all,
He forgives and keeps forgiving
    Try again... just stand up tall.

Gertrude B. McClain

*My help is
from the Lord
who made heaven
and earth.*
Ps. 121:2

Thank You. . .

Precious God, great and good
We thank You for our daily food,
Given with all gracious love
From heaven's storehouse
Up above.

Our needs You do daily meet
With tenderness, pure and sweet.
Gracious God, we thank You dear,
That in Your heart You hold
Us near.

Elizabeth Mc Clung

Life's Duet

How happy! How happy!
Our daily life will be
If played as a duet
With Christ, In harmony.
Enhanced by the Maestro
Of every human heart
Life becomes beautiful
As we play our small part.

Sr. Mary Gemma Brunke

*G*ive thanks to the Lord of lords...
To him who alone does
great wonders...
Ps. 136:3, 4

Each Day Is Filled With Miracles

Each day is filled with miracles
   That many do not see,
While others take for granted
   The buds upon the tree.

Some never see the sunrise
   Or gaze upon the stars,
Nor do they search the winter skies
   For Jupiter and Mars.

Some haven't seen the golden leaves
   Beneath an autumn moon,
Or wandered through a field of dreams
   On a sunny day in June.

Some never see beneath the snow
   The promise of a rose,
Or often wonder like a child
   Just why a firefly glows.

Each day is filled with miracles
   Wherever we may trod,
But many take for granted
   The simple gifts of God.

            Clay Harrison

Mother's Home

I visited the old homestead
The house is empty now,
I hear the echoes in the hall
Her presence too, somehow.

The walls, they speak of memories
And, in each room I find,
A story here of yesteryear
That lives still in my mind.

No… nothing here can help me
Recapture days of yore,
Or… bring back the days, emotions -
That here, we lived before.

We all know an empty house
Can be a home no more
Until it's filled with love and souls
As it had been before.

James Joseph Huesgen

My Mountain Home

The moon is full the woods are deep
    Below the world is lost in sleep,
The air is crisp, so cool and clear
    Far off the singing stream I hear.

Just God and I together roam
    This wilderness, my mountain home,
My soul is born again where He
    Does seem so close and dear to me.

The nighthawk sails the starry sky
    The soft wind hums her lullaby,
The black bear and the old raccoon
    Must find a den for sleeping soon.

For not too long from now I know
    The mountain will be hushed in snow,
A wonderland these hills will be
    As far as any man can see.

And I, by God, so very blest
    Before the fire will sit and rest,
In warmth and peace I'll have no care
    With those I love beside me there.

Kate Watkins Furman

A Winter Day

The air was filled with winter
With snowflakes soft and white,
The air was thick and heavy
With winter's sweet delight,
How lovely was the morning
With sparkling snowflakes gay,
The trees decked out in splendor
Along the country way.

The world was gay with winter
Yet sunshine bright as gold,
Shone down in quiet splendor
Despite the winter's cold,
The early hours of dawning
Brought peace and gladness rare,
My heart aglow with winter
Around me everywhere.

The world was charmed by winter
WIth Jack Frost here again,
To paint his sparkling pictures
Upon my window pane,
All sparkling in the sunlight
They shone in bright array,
I saw the hand of winter
That blessed this lovely day.

The snowflakes danced with winter
And brought a quiet thrill,
A bit of white to treasure
Atop an autumn hill,
No doubt, but this was winter
The evidence was there,
Amidst the twirling snowflakes
A winter day so fair.

Garnett Ann Schultz

God Bless The Work!

God bless the work that lies before each hand,
God's blessing be on all that we have done!
For what is fame or gift or treasure grand
If His approving smile we have not won!

God strengthen us when crosses come to stay,
When shadows close around each heart and home.
God guide our souls when light seems far away
And all the wide world's waves are white with foam.

In body and in soul God keep us strong
To toil for Him and never fail through fear;
This is our wish, our prayer the whole day long;
God bless the work each hour of every year.

Brian O'Higgins

*Cast your burden
upon the Lord and
He will sustain you.*
Ps. 55:22

Grant Me Thy Reward. . .

Sometimes I feel I can't go on;
Oh, lead me, Precious Lord --
Come, take my weary hand in Thine,
And grant me Thy reward...

Sometimes I feel I can't go on;
Give me Thy strength, dear Lord --
Without Thy courage and Thy will,
There is naught I can afford...

Sometimes I feel I can't go on;
I'm tired, Lord, and weak --
Oh hold me safe in Thy embrace,
For Thy blessed hope I seek...

Sometimes I feel I can't go on;
Uplift me, Precious Lord --
Come tarry with me, night and day,
And may Thou be adored...

Sometimes I feel I can't go on;
Restore my faith, oh Lord --
Bless me with everlasting peace,
And grant me Thy reward!

Hope C. Oberhelman

*...he who sows virtue
has a sure reward.*
Prov. 11:18

I'm Not Alone

My cross is not too heavy,
My road is not too rough
Because God walks beside me
And to know this is enough...
And though I get so lonely
I know I'm not alone
For the Lord God is my Father
And He loves me as His own...
So though I'm tired and weary
And I wish my race were run
God will only terminate it
When my work on earth is done...
So let me stop complaining
About my load of care
For God will always lighten it
When it gets too much to bear...
And if He does not ease my load
He will give me strength to bear it
For God in love and mercy
Is always near to share it.

Helen Steiner Rice

*God is our refuge and
strength, a very present
help in trouble.*
Psalms 46:1

Used with permission of
The Helen Steiner Rice Foundation
Cincinnati, OH 45202

If

If God can paint a sunset
And color autumn's trees,
If He can make the stars shine,
And perfume springtime's breeze,
If God can set the gold sun
In smiling skies of blue,
Friend, do you ever ponder
What He can do for you?

If God can chart the course of
The geese as winter nears,
If He can clothe the lilies
That in the field appear,
If God cares for the sparrows
And watches over all,
Friend, will He not meet your needs,
And harken to your call?

If God can hold the whole world
Within His mighty hand,
If storm-tossed seas obey Him
And cease at His command,
If God can make a rainbow
When clouds their work are through -
He's in control of our lives.
I know He cares. Don 't you?

Beverly J. Anderson

Visit From A Friend

Come in, my friend, I'll take your coat.
Let's sit and chat a while.
This snowy day will seem less drear
Illumined by your smile.
My friend sits down and draws a chair
Close to the fire's rouge glow.
We talk of hobbies, family, home,
And nearby folks we know.
Our world expands beyond the hearth
To church, the county, state.
We reminiscence of bygone days
And childhood fun relate.
We laugh at pranks we used to play,
Snow sculpture we would make,
Recall schoolmates, loved pets, old books,
Ice skating on the lake.
The pleasant visit slips away.
Although our time must end,
My wintry heart has lost its chill
Enkindled by a friend.

Louise Pugh Corder

The Divine Key

Step by step I journey onward
Sometimes truly unaware
That deep within my human temple
God resides and wants to share.
Share the wealth, the joy, the beauty
Plus a mountain high and more
But before we can reap a harvest
We must first unlock the door.
We must come in faith believing
As God waits for our gentle knock
But wonders why we delayed in coming
When the door we could unlock.
Perhaps you waited due to blindness
And filled with doubt you could not see
But now that your eyes are open
Oh, what glory there shall be.
Like a glistening inner mirror
Like a treasure that's been found
You are awe struck by the beauty
Of the jeweled-gifts all around.
All these gifts He will lavish freely
Without effort on our part
We must only keep believing
And God will then unlock our heart.

Chris Zambernard

I Have Faith

I have faith in the new day that's coming,
in the things that I know I shall do;

I have faith that there'll be something
lovely for me,
and I've faith in myself, have you?

I believe that our God will watch over,
and I know that He'll always take care;

And if things go wrong, we shall still have
a song
and a happiness always to share.

That's why I have faith in tomorrow,
though today might be lonely and blue;

My best I shall give, in each new day I live,
and my own faith shall carry me through.

Garnett Ann Schultz